Super Babies!

Dona Herweck Rice

Publishing Credits

Rachelle Cracchiolo, M.S.Ed., *Publisher*
Conni Medina, M.A.Ed., *Managing Editor*
Nika Fabienke, Ed.D., *Content Director*
Véronique Bos, *Creative Director*
Shaun N. Bernadou, *Art Director*
Seth Rogers, *Editor*
John Leach, *Assistant Editor*
Courtney Roberson, *Senior Graphic Designer*

Image Credits: All images from iStock and/or Shutterstock.

Library of Congress Cataloging-in-Publication Data

Names: Rice, Dona, author.
Title: Super babies / Dona Herweck Rice.
Description: Huntington Beach, CA : Teacher Created Materials, [2019] |
Identifiers: LCCN 2018029727 (print) | LCCN 2018033714 (ebook) | ISBN 9781493899487 | ISBN 9781493898749
Subjects: LCSH: Readers (Primary)
Classification: LCC PE1119 (ebook) | LCC PE1119 .R467 2019 (print) | DDC 428.6/2--dc23
LC record available at https://lccn.loc.gov/2018029727

Teacher Created Materials
5301 Oceanus Drive
Huntington Beach, CA 92649-1030
www.tcmpub.com

ISBN 978-1-4938-9874-9

Printed in China
Nordica.082018.CA21800936

What if a 

baby

could 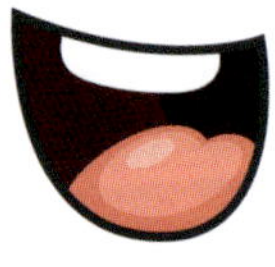 ?

talk

What if a 

baby

could  ?

cook

What if a  baby

could  surf ?

What if a  baby

could  drive ?

What if a 

baby

could  ?

sing

What if a 

baby

could  ?

type

What if a  baby

could  read ?

What if a  baby

could  dance ?

What if a  baby

could  ride ?

What if a 

baby

could ?

fly

High-Frequency Words

New Words

could if
what

Review Word

a